The He
Sp
Vol

MW01531125

Editorial Staff

Mick Kennedy
Founder, Editor

Amy Fox-Angerer
Managing Editor

Ted Higgs   Yvonne Morris
Associate Editors

Deena Lilygren
Fiction Editor

Editorial Assistants
Poetry
Matt Brennan   Tasha Cotter   Michael Coyle

Fiction
Sue Ballard   Jan Nemes
Robert Villanueva   Barry Williams

Secretary
Sandi Howard

Technical Support
Barry Williams

Cover
Untitled (Oil on canvas)

Alan Vance

THR

Elizabethtown Community and Technical College
600 College Street Road
Elizabethtown, KY

Elizabethtown
Community & Technical College

© **2019 The Heartland Review Press**

ISSN 2473-9545

ISBN: 978-0-9996868-5-0

The Heartland Review is published with generous funds from KCTCS and Elizabethtown Community and Technical College president's office, as well as donations from friends, contributors, and contest entrants. We want to thank everyone for the continued support of this journal.

To submit go to:

The Heartland Review Submittable

To subscribe, visit our website

$4.00/issue $7.00/year

Printed by Ingram-Spark

Contributors

Younger Artists

Editor's Notes

As we near the twentieth year of the Joy Bale Boone Poetry Prize, we are reminded of the many marvelous authors who have peopled our pages. More importantly, we say thanks to all of those who entered the contest and fell short of prizes or publications. The currency that we expend toward contest recognition, purchasing others' books, and, more commonly, just to have an editor consider our work for publication is daunting. However, our transactions in the community of writers keeps that pulse steady. Unfortunately, for the most part, the larger world does not—cannot—value the ART that we in the writerly world witness each time we peel back a new (or used) cover. So, let us revel in our commerce in our self-sustainability.

This year's judge Jed Myers, a poetic force indeed, and a truly magnificent human being, chose the recipients of 2019 prize. Of them, he wrote:

Michael Lasater's "'Documentary' is an irreverent and reverent poem. It first documents the artist's funny and sad artifices with water. Then the poem takes us out of itself and "home" to origins that cannot be 'framed' or 'faked.' While we seem to be lifted away from the water of art, we wind up where the crows 'flood' over us, where we 'crouch hidden in the river's western bend,' in the water of life. I am stirred complexly by this piece, and find myself wondering what this poet's other works might offer."

Hannah Yoest's "'Sonset' is a poem that plays bravely with truth's darknesses. It will not bow to any comforting givens, no matter how 'bruised' that leaves the world. And as much as this is a work of disillusionment, it resolves in a sunset we suspect is the more beautiful for this implicit renunciation of the unreal 'promise of ecstasy outlined in neon....'"

Chera Hammond's "'Dear Disease' embodies an experience of intimate entrapment within the dual identity, the 'we,' that long illness can engender. There's a strong sense here of being hidden inside the 'dome of demands' that is the disease. This poet has neither named nor depicted the particular malady and yet has been able to bring us inside its 'bell.' The poem stands to help us hear the human presence 'ringing against / this prison's walls....'"

These poems add to the textual fluidity of our annual poetry prize that Joy would have applauded.

On another note, The Heartland Review Press traveled to Maryville College in Maryville, TN – which is celbrating its 200th anniversary – to launch Ted Higgs' newest collection of poems. As part of the event, creative writing students and their instructor Chirstina Seymour were invited to read in the Blueberry Farm Gallery, surrounded by new paintings by Alan Vance, studio professor at Elizabethtown Community and Technical College (ECTC), an example of which adorns this issue's cover.

The authors from Maryville College join ECTC student authors in this issue to complement the extrordinary pieces from the finalsists and award winners of the 2019 Joy Bale Boone Poetry Prize and to continue the advocacy of young artists' creations.

mk, Editor

Libby Falk Jones

Flight

I've been there, once or twice, about a thousand feet
above the fields and farms and hills of East Kentucky
where wind whirs outside the cockpit window
and the plane dips its wings in homage to the land.

Above the hills and farms and fields of East Kentucky,
sometimes flocks of snow geese honk and clatter,
dipping their wings toward land as I stand watching,
my wishes drifting skyward like cumulus clouds.

Sometimes I hear geese flapping and honking.
How small I must seem to them – a strange sort of tree
whose wishes drift skyward to weave among the clouds.
In their eyes, only patterns of water, light, earth.

How small and strange I must seem, a milkweed exploded,
if they have eyes beyond wings' rhythms, wind's whir,
for the patterns, shadows, beneath them. With them
I've been there, up there, more than a thousand feet.

Gary Beaumier

The Migratory Habits of Dreams in Late Autumn

During the first cycle you may visit your childhood home
and they will all be there as though still alive
and there may be steaming pots
on the stove and your mother will turn to you and smile
as you will sit in a chair too big for you
while your dog settles his head in your lap

during your second cycle you dream of leaves
that have loosed themselves and drift and tumble
in quiet descent and with each you
give them the names of those who have passed
and whisper sweet prayers as your rake
gathers great drifts of them to a burn pile,
their smoky incense carried up to intersect
with a flock of birds

And in the final cycle
your breathing will slow and lengthen
as your breast heaves and settles
again ever slower and someone will read to you
as you feel the press of their weight on the bed
they will read soft words from a children's book
word by word by word
and pages will rustle like leaves
and there will be no need of anything
– all is said and done –
and you will be loosed
to rise and fall at the same time
as the earth recedes
you drift higher and are carried south
while a snow accumulates and whitens
everything below

Jayne Marek

Walking into Cloud

at the top of the hill, in a bowl of morning sunlight, I pass
a yard of yellow sunflowers then walk into cloud

in late July, early fog asleep over the Strait rising to my eye
level: unseen on the water below, Native canoes slip

through the silver like otters, like orcas, like eagles:
yesterday the canoes came around the point and were

invited to land by local tribespeople, and all night the canoes
held their carved heads above the shoreline watching

the gibbous moon bring in the tide nearly to their breasts
while the Native camps a mile away drummed

and danced and ate after another leg of the journey toward
the tribal gathering, a few more days' paddle southward,

as the canoes in the dark waited for their families to rest,
the carved logs embodying spirits of all the people

of forests and water and sky who know they are of this earth
and who can travel forward with unseeing sense, so well

do they know: on hilltop streets I walk quietly and hear
the bell buoy out in the channel speak its word, muffled,

and in a tangle of bushes a mixed flock of birds
chatters to each other about the spiderwebs and bugs

they find; one tiny gray bird jumps to an outer branch
to look at me, its body shorter than my little finger:

it probably thinks itself more important than a human;
I suppose it is, surely at least here in this

thicket and among its group, this bushtit with its fellow
foragers the chestnut-backed chickadees and kinglets:

I walk on past a scattering of wildflowers with orange poppies
still folded against the chill, the bachelor buttons

knotted by a few laces of fog: here I can turn into a stand
of Douglas firs and brush, and find a lode of thimbleberry

bushes lining a path; in shade and mist glow three or four
spots of red, delicious to see and to taste; I am glad

to have them and to notice that many berries already
have been eaten by the woods people, perhaps those birds

that greeted me a few minutes earlier: I can no longer
hear the channel bell but it will be there, dipping

the sides of its platform into the low morning waves
again, again, moving like paddles, as tide carries

all of its beings, above and below it, and those listening
from high above, toward daylight opening in the east

Jed Myers

Late Broadcast

We saw the bright blurs arc over
Damascus on our little screen, flashes
in a grainy dark low-resolution

scene so indistinct one could question
its deaths. Sound caught a loudspeaker
call to prayer. An evening in spring.

Time when the lilacs here turn luminous
in the long beams. I wanted to walk
out with you as the dark came down,

back to those lookout steps by the lake
where we first kissed, and kiss. The night
like any, it could be our city candle-lit

under plummeting tail-fires. I hope
we'd slow-dance to the thuds as the blasts come
close, glowing matter in careless celebration.

Or would you have us do something else,
not this late broadcast of our body-selves
in embrace, inhaling the dust of the shambles?

Love's last dips and turns where the light
can escape, our hands where the stars can see them
on each other's waist — what could be better?

Here we still are, where the bees came once more
today to hover and adore the irises
unfurling their purple entranceways.

The star witnesses in their light-years' distance
will eventually see our cheeks touch,
see our invisible trust in their telescopes,

though all our poems have burned. And if
there are no such lenses, a poem will once
have said we saw more than could be written

when we looked inches across the sudden
blizzard of ash, in these eyes.

Honorable Mention 2019 Joy Bale Boone Poetry Prize

Michael Lasater

West of Wichita

... as much the certainty of unknowing as
the relentless subtraction of growing old.

My friend writes: I will pray for you
even though
    I know you do not believe.

Yes.

    And yet those who cannot believe
may also pray—pray out of sheer unbelief perhaps—
pray to no one, to a fable, an empty room—or
pray to the wind, one of the old gods, the messenger
of prayer—a god with breath and body, a god
    you can touch and hear.

Unbelief has its rituals, its priests.

Blinds half shut against the late afternoon sun,
we sing to ourselves as we prepare a dinner
we've enjoyed a thousand evenings before.
There will be wine – that much endures, at least –
and later music – Schumann – circling –
turning – color swirling –
                vanishing –

Listen.

This morning I dreamt we had another child – a boy.
First desire, then form, face and flesh –
then a voice, laughing as children always laugh –
running to me – father –
              a mirage like him.

Linda Flaherty Haltmaier

Morning Fix

I eat Sylvia Plath for breakfast,
between bites of toast,
burnt edges
raining soot on the page,
a linea nigra forming
in the belly of the book.

Her red tulips and bright needles
eclipse the other senses,
and the toast,
even the jam,
have no taste,
words fill my mouth,
crowd my teeth,
my tongue a limp, stunned animal.

Images race down my arms and legs
on paths an addict treads,
highways of chi in full flame,
pricking knots of ganglia
and unsuspecting toes
with wonder
and heart ache.

Chera Hammonds

Dear Disease

Before I knew it, I was living in rooms with you
like you were the partner I had chosen.
And every decision was Ours.
What should we do today?
What should we wear? you ask.
I wear my jacket collar up to block the wind.
You walk beside me, rubber-soled,
to the supermarket, where you take out of the basket
what I put in. Aren't you a fine dictator of appetites.
We sit on the couch and flip through the channels,
a rolodex of noise and want.
We argue as every couple might,
until I know what you will say
even before you say it.
Shut up, just shut up, I want to tell you,
but I am too polite, and you always get your way.
In the mornings, I wake up with you.
You are in the mirror, framed over spit in the sink,
looking back at me expectantly.
Everywhere I look, in fact, there you are waiting,
impenetrable, inescapable, a dome of demands.
I abide. Do you hear me? I am still here.
I am ringing against
this prison's walls with one note,
like the heart of a bell.

Tim Menees

Thirty

When they announced the closing of Spruce Landing High School, Abbott "A-Bomb" Brickle fumed to the school board, "We're not sending our kids up to no goddam Boxley!" As if Boxley were Baghdad. Maribeth recounted A-Bomb's outburst on the editorial page and in her weekly column, but changed "goddam" to "goll dang" because this was the *Spruce Landing Mail*, not *The New Yorker*.

She and her husband Donnie owned the *Mail*, "The Whole Kaboodle" as he put in the masthead. She said, "This is as close we'll ever get to *The New York Times*."

They had owned the paper for twenty-two years, flirted with selling it, but hung on after a look-see trip to Dogfish Island. Now Maribeth was publishing the paper's final edition.

She and Donnie had read that the island's weekly was on the market, a "high-power, popular and award-winning newspaper" and suggested they visit cousin Shelby. Shelby and his wife had left Spruce Landing several years earlier and moved to the island "to see if it was true about young men going west." They'd visited Maribeth and Donnie a couple times and gushed over the island and the mountains and the Dunginess crab. Maribeth said, "It's time to see Gatesville."

Donnie had taught science and was the school's newspaper advisor at Spruce Landing High but left when economics threatened its closing and teachers would end up at distant schools. He told Maribeth he'd get a high-powered job at Boeing. She said, "Or scootering around Amazon."

They flew to Seattle and rented a cottage for a week on Dogfish on a hill overlooking the sound. Shelby drove them over the local roads, past the local beaches, out to Lighthouse Point, and back into town for lunch at *Le Belle Île* cafe. They toured the paper. The *Weekly Islander* office wasn't much larger than the *Mail*, but it was spiffed up with skylights, paintings of old steam ferryboats, and Indian art. Although the island was growing the owners, a couple from Tacoma, were moving to Hawaii. The paper came with two employees: a rouged woman named Rose who talked as though she were a Seattle grande doyenne (she wasn't), and the owner's sister-in-law Pansy whose *nom du journal* was "Island Sweet" who wrote a humor column Maribeth called "one big sugar cookie."

They looked over the office, back issues, ad revenues and circulation figures. Rose asked where they were from, and Maribeth said, West Virginia, she looked as if Maribeth had said Chaw Tobacky, Alabama. She said, "Truth be told, we're not looking forward to the change."

Maribeth said, "No one does."

As Donnie and Maribeth left, the women said more bragging than embracing, "Welcome to God's Country."

Maribeth said, "Thank you from Almost Heaven."

During their stay, they took the boat to Seattle, and on one of the three days it didn't rain, drove part way up to Mount Rainier then had dinner on the Seattle waterfront. She said, "Folks treat Rainier like an animal – 'It's out today!'" They rarely spotted it.

They decided to pass. She told her sons, "We were just more fish out of water." To Shelby she said, "It's crowded out here, and it's surely alive, but we know Spruce Landing and the hills of Appalachia, the Potomac River, even the worn-out coal mines. We know nothing about geoducks." They returned to Spruce Landing" and writing stories, shooting photos, selling ads, editing PR handouts, doing page layout and printing the twelve-page paper. Donnie named himself CEO ("The only way I'll ever be one"). Maribeth was publisher and editor-in-chief. They still divvied up opening mail, making coffee and tidying up.

At one time the paper numbered sixteen pages, then came the soaring cost of newsprint, shrinking ad lineage, dwindling subscriptions and, even up in the mountains of western Maryland, the Internet.

"Look at us," she told Donnie. "All of us. "We're shrinking away to nothing," she told Donnie. We won't be any bigger than a neighborhood freebie. The only one left will be *The New York Times* with a zone edition for every city.

Indeed, the *Mail*, like the town, was dying, dying like Donnie did two years ago from a massive heart attack that left him dead before the EMT crew arrived.

Tomorrow with its last issue Maribeth will pronounce now the eight-page *Spruce Landing Mail* dead.

"I don't see why you can't keep it going," their son DJ said on the phone from Washington, D.C. "Where are people going to get their news?"

"The old-fashioned way," Maribeth said. "Gossip."

"What are you going to do?" asked older son David, whom Maribeth suspected was thinking: *Now we've gotta take care of Mom.* She told him his father would have done like other ex-CEOs who get axed – claimed he wanted to spend more time with his family." David said, "Who? Dad?"

David admonished her again for following the McLanes and the Breyers and the Sonnenbirds and grabbing lakefront property when it was bargain basement and before it turned into million-dollar write-offs for the one-percenters from Baltimore and D.C. and Pittsburgh. "So what?" Donnie had told him, "We're still OK." Then the cost of news-print went nuts and and the local supermarket went bust which caused a plummet in ad money. "I've got some irons in the fire."

"Like what?" DJ asked.

"Wagon master."

When he called this time, David said, even more unconvincingly, "Can we help?"

Maribeth said, "I'm working a deal on Kickstarter – "

"Gallows humor."

"I'm up to forty dollars. Another twenty grand oughta do it." Silence. "At least our house is paid off." Silence. She still called it "our house" even though she was a widow, a word she hated. Widows were tall, gaunt crones with thin lips, dressed in black, faces behind black veils, forever unsmiling, eyes like ravens, silent and bitter.

When Donnie died, she feared she could never endure another night. Why her? What had she done to anyone? What had Donnie? She went to grief counseling but she was never one for groups that prolonged agony. She got more succinct wisdom from a friend whose husband had died three years earlier: "We lost all our secrets, those special signs and signals and looks, our own language. You'll move on and maybe learn another."

She found a replacement for Donnie, at least to help at the *Mail.* Kendra was an accountant who had been laid off at the paper mill. She was smart and eager and knew spread sheets and computers and how to keep their finances, if not in the black, at least "in the gray."

As for the lake, her parents had, in fact, snagged a parcel of bargain-basement lakefront property which, after their mother died of cancer, she had stood to inherit when her father died. They were optimistic even though Dad was often at odds with his daughter over her editorials. So was David, but never said much because he'd moved to Easton, Penn-sylvania, where he taught college chemistry, and even though the paper arrived every week by snail mail, he was too distant to make a fuss.

Maribeth and Donnie had paid off their mortgage because houses in

Spruce Landing had always come cheap. They lived in what some called "the silk-stocking district," meaning their hillside street had recently been paved and their neighbors kept up the lawns, never junking them up with old house trailers and chunks of machinery. Spruce Landing sat spread over two lumpy mountains, basically steep hills, a collection of aging frame houses, some behind chipped vinyl siding or insulbrick, and newer brick or stone ramblers. Several sat along the Potomac River which was not much wider than a two-lane road.

The school had indeed closed to the ire of A-Bomb & Company, and the children of Greater Spruce Landing, now boasting a population of two-thousand, were being bused to Boxley with no apparent damage to their collective psyche. The local theater on Main Street was long closed, as were two of the three bars, the barbershop, the dime store, the florist and soda shop. The pizza place had survived. A mile down the road Food City and its six-store strip mall that had helped cause the collapse stood empty.

"They said Food City was here to say," Sprucers said. "Just goes to show."

The three-man police department had been disbanded, turning what crime there was – at present a growing and deadly heroin addiction – over to the county sheriff. The local Catholic priest now dashed among four parishes. The Moose Club was hurting and so was A-Bomb's Vets Club. Freight trains hauling two-hundred hopper cars mounded with coal still rumbled and clanked through town every few hours, but Amtrak had long ago abandoned its stop at nearby Rollins.

The paper mill, the only industry in town, had been cutting back, especially after it bought plants in Mississippi and Brazil, while bashing Washington over air-pollution laws. Maribeth had to handle that one gingerly. Her uncle and cousin had retired from the mill and she had worked there for two summers. She wrote: "We need our jobs *and* our lungs. Our government is us, folks, it's not Russians sweeping across our land raping and pillaging." (This was before Vladimir Putin rode across *his* land bareback.) The company mostly ignored her editorials, holding to an unpublished corporate policy: "Pick your fights."

"When I write some of this stuff," she told Donnie, "I feel like I should be wearing black patent-leather fuck-me pumps."

Several readers, including A-Bomb, crafted lengthy screeds, and if she shortened them for space, they attacked her for "elite, liberal news censorship."

"'Liberal news,'" Donnie scoffed. "I'm a vet, and I've always voted Republican. A-Bomb and them, they all know it."

Alone in the silence of her bedroom she talks to Donnie like a true believer, but never waits for an answer or a sign. She told him on Monday, "You oughta see this place now."

As the town's fortunes slid further into the river, it tried to reinvent itself, first as an arts center. Mayor Frender hired a three-person search committee and found a painter named Caprice in Hagerstown who moved into the abandoned florist's shop for twenty dollars a month plus a percentage of any sales. She stayed a year, produced a series of acrylics based on animal and plant dreams. When none sold she packed up their dreams and hers and returned to Hagerstown.

During a public hearing chaired by Mayor Frender, for "some honest brain-storming," the Belanders who lived near Maribeth urged the town to get a call center. Mrs. Belander said that people hated the airlines and getting some guy in Pakistan who calls himself "Josh." Mr. Belander said, "You can't talk to them like you can Americans, important stuff like football." They told the committee, "Other places are doing it — parts of Texas which are dirt poor. The Republicans are America First and they'll give us the cash."

The committee said they'd look into it.

Their local Congressman, while loudly GOP, didn't live nearby and was a no-show.

Mrs. Belander wasn't through. "While you're at it," she said, get Congress to give us a big old FBI center like Robert Bird did over there in Clarksburg."

The committee said they'd look into it.

It quickly swung to another extreme, as Mayor Frender put it: "All aboard the high-tech express!" Like what? the committee wondered, still nursing its wounds from Caprice. "A startup. It can mushroom into five-hundred jobs. Get a name like Smashbash or Lipsock or Torquedoll."

Norma Alderson who worked at Hoppy's, the last saloon standing on Main Street, said, "I read get Google and property values go sky high."

The committee wrote to Google in Mountain View, California. A corporate PR exec, "probably a twenty-two-year old geek," said Maribeth, wrote back. He thanked them, but Spruce Landing wasn't in their expansion plans at the moment.

Mayor Frender proposed a floating casino. "Floating casino?" scoffed A-Bomb, turning to the crowd for support. "There ain't enough water in the river to float a canoe. Plus the government'll make us get Indians to run it and we don't have any." The mayor promised the search committee would find one. "Plus," said A-Bomb, "Coal Mountain already has a casino."

Too far away, said hizzoner. "We could resettle Syrians here – we got vacant houses." When that stalled he said, "We want business and they start businesses."

Mr. Sonnenbird snorted, "What kind, car bombs?"

"Restaurants."

The small city of River Mills an hour away had gone through this ringer. A fairly vibrant arts community got going, but when the art scene slowed, it turned to the Coal Mountain Casino then for insurance another sure-fire savior: prisons.

"They also got," said Norma, "prisoners' families who move in with bigger issues than buying paintings."

A-Bomb wrote the paper and said Spruce Landing was so far up the sticks it was a perfect place for a prison – "We retrofit our old mine shafts . . . "

Following that meeting Maribeth wrote in her weekly column in the *Mail*:

> This has slid from brain-storming to brain dead. It reminds us of something we heard recently: "Want to know how to make God laugh? Tell Him your plans." Life and death can't be scripted. They're organic.

That set off A-Bomb against "the liberal agenda of buying organic over regular onions," and climate change and death squads.

As she typed her final column for the *Mail*, she told Kendra that A-Bomb's letter would actually be funny if he could get past putting prisons in mine shafts. She was finishing it up Monday for Wednesday's edition when the phone rang.

"The U.S. Cavalry," Kendra said.

It was Corporal Weller, her contact at the Maryland State Police with word that Naomi Meecham, a local high-school cheerleader, had been killed that morning when an eighty-year-old driver strayed over the center line and hit her head on.

"Goddamn it, Bruce, that's all we need," she muttered into the phone as she typed the information. "Joey and Leah are going to be frigging ruined." She heard herself breathing hard into the receiver.

The paper had been set but this had to run on Page One and above the fold. "I trust," she told Donnie as she looked at the florescent lights, "you'd heartily agree." She was a mess. She recalled Eddie Ormon, a sixteen-year-old who played baseball and the trumpet at the high school six years earlier. He'd coped with depression and hanged himself in his parents' garage. When she wanted to soften the obit, they said, no, print the details. By the time the final paper came out, the town was figuratively draped in black. St. Adolph's Bereavement Committee sent food over to Naomi's parents, and made sure the nave of the airy high-ceilinged church would be filled with flowers.

Below Naomi's obit and photo, yet miles apart, she ran a sampling of the paper's past stories: pollution in the Potomac River, a WWII vet awarded the Medal of Honor fifty years after D-Day, railroad safety after a dozen tank cars derailed with two careening into the river, and a barnburner on industrial missteps at the mill, which landed it a national award and a threatened suit from Corporate. She reprinted a few memorable letters to the editor, including one from A-Bomb which accused Donnie of "a three-way with Nancy Pelosi and Sarah Palin and not being able to do anything about it." He charged Mayor Frender with "taking enough bribes from the mill union to put a Russki oligarch to shame," and told Maribeth to "get a real job like Anne Coulter."

In a page-one farewell column, she wrote, in bold face as she sometimes did:

> To turn Mark Twain on his head, the report
> of the death of the *Spruce Landing Mail* is
> not an exaggeration. Folks, we expire this
> morning. Now we can, as did Tom and Huck,
> watch our own funeral.
> It should come as no surprise. We're not
> the first newspaper in America to lock its
> doors nor will we be the last. Newspapers
> reflect their communities and Spruce Landing
> has been slipping away. Like countless small
> towns we are dying. We are ignored by the
> rich who buy McMansions on the lake and
> scoff at the rest of us. Cities in the
> Rust Belt are seeking resurrection. The first
> blows for all of us come from the malls and

followed by Walmart wearing an executioner's
mask. Our children leave. We age and die.
Sometimes, tragically, so does our youth.
(See our story on beautiful Naomi Meecham.)
As for the Mail, spiraling newsprint costs,
plunging ad revenue and dwindling circulation
have taken their toll. So has the Internet.
Newspapers across the nation have folded.
Others come out three days a week. All are
cutting staff.
None of us has conquered the Internet. Neither
has radio or TV. Maybe we will one day arise
like Lazarus. Maybe.
Until then, we thank all of you and we will
miss every reader.
Some of you will mourn our passing, others
might jitterbug on our grave. One person has
told us he would spit on it.
In a bit of ancient newspaperese that
reporters onced used to end their stories, we
close with a simple: 30

She used the editorial "we" but meant "I".

In the six months following Naomi Meecham's death, Spruce Land-ing buried a high-school boy, a father in his forties, a fifty-year-old fore-man at the mill and five seniors, including another WWII vet who was one week short of turning one hundred.

The four women on the bereavement committee, down from a dozen, still come through with lunch and flowers, but Maribeth doesn't figure they will bake their casseroles much longer. She told Donnie, "Kids, and I mean also kids in their forties, no longer bother with be-reavement committees, church, the Masons, the Odd Fellows and the Rainbow Girls."

And her lake cottage was no longer a lock.

Her dad married an octogenarian lady named Beezie, who dyed her hair blonde and wore glossy magenta lipstick. She and Maribeth shared a mutual and avid dislike. During a Thanksgiving Day dinner argument over welfare, Beezie called her a communist, and in the privacy of the upstairs hall, Maribeth called Beezie "a gold-digging racist slut." She and Frank learned Dad named Beezie executrix, and the new will said zip about any lake property.

22

She threatened a court challenge. Frank filed suit. Beezie dug in her stiletto heels. At her age, Maribeth grumped.

Frank told Maribeth, "I oughta sue *you!*"

Maribeth called her cousin Shelby and said, "I might just move out to that Dogfish Island of yours after all."

She looked skyward and said, "Donnie, why . . . never mind."

***

Today she misses her readers from a bungalow in Cambridge on Maryland's Eastern Shore. She tells friends, "We're sticking our toe in the Bay."

She means "I".

She has never named her mysterious grave spitter which has left Spruce Landing guessing and gossiping. In a Vets Club pool started by its new bartender Norma Alderson, A-Bomb sits on his usual barstool, third from the end, and holds an insurmountable, run-out-the-clock 22-8 lead.

Christina Seymour

Fervent Beast

The missing girl got lost in a high, colorful wind
she thought was a love song.

Her plastic-rimmed glasses in Evidence
are the town's promise to protect the misguided—

her hair in the pictures, half yellow and sweat—
my promise to look for burns underneath.

On the purple pond, I boat toward the island
which sends the mother heron toward my head.

I want to say, I am not interested in your nest—
I am a routine, a nothing-new. I am found.

Every day, I curve on the bed to fit my hound,
encircled in herself. She paws my mouth by dawn,

a private, universal hunger. To her, I am a lottery.
To the missing girl I've summoned on the news

and, now, parade in my daydream while watering the grass,
I am not even an idea.

First Place 2019 Joy Bale Boone Poetry Prize

Michael Lasater

Documentary

In my film the poet (my friend Jim)
first appears framed in late September rain.

It's all faked, of course.

Armed with a garden hose, my giggling assistant
deftly showers the artist's kitchen window –
for his close-up, Jim holds a steaming kettle to fog
its glazed panes – and I have purchased the sound
of thunder (British thunder!) so you the viewer soon
are swept into my quick little stream of careful lies.

Jim trusts me to perjure on his behalf,
and I swear I will not let him down.

Sheltering my camera, I wait in mist for
a single drop to form and fall from
a barbed wire fence. I pay a friend
(whom I later fire) for rights to watch
his bathroom faucet drip. I freeze ice,
mix drinks, water lawns, scrub out sinks,
go trout fishing, take a shower.

This is Art!

I get a grant.
My film is broadcast.
I win an award.

In early winter I return home –
my father and I drive out to the Ninnescah where
together we have hunted time upon time.

In the evening the crows fly in to roost.
Trailing their scout they flood over the catalpas
where we crouch hidden in the river's western bend.

I look at the water. The Ninnescah moves quietly.
Above its face the crows speed and cry,
skimming the dusk in their ancient black ritual.

The river calls them by name.

25

Patrick Sylvain

Jujubean

For J. LB

With gritted teeth and chili-pepper eyes, you watched
My boat of desire sail into the horizontal abyss
As your heart pumped sorrow in its own harbor.

What you harbor toward me is an iron oar, cutting.
But our distance is an ocean of silence, and no number
Of oarlocks can clamp me back to your shore.

Years of cavernous pain, forming a grotto of guilt
Inside my skull. How could I go on not penning a mea culpa?
You were once the essence, never cheap sex. A blue Jay

Beyond the exquisite gift of beauty. You wanted the bonding
Of rings, the cradling of heirs. I was too young for husbandry.
You believed in providence and sortilege was trashing a good love.

I cannot kneel before you, siphon the pus of grief that
Festers your heart, but I can script my regrets into verse
For the song unsung upon the altar of "everlasting."

We heard the angels sing, and we intoxicated ourselves
With laughter (I remember, you loved cherry Pinot Noir).
But, you were too thin-skinned for my taste.

Instead, my hastened departure, like a rough seaman,
Brought waves of suffering onto your flawless coastline.
I was the first to have taken you to the rough seas.

You wanted for us to remain a tight cluster:
Conico-cylindrical, voluptuous, like the pinot grapes
You loved. That would have been a viticultural hazard.

Kory Wells

All Things Are a Darkness
—James Dickey

Days when the house was empty,
   everyone in the fields but
      us kids, the granny-woman

      from down the way would appear
  on our porch. She smelled of soot
and sour milk but most of all

ham biscuits. We'd let her in.
   After our bellies were full,
      she'd lure us behind the door,

      show us how to charm a stream
  of milk from an ax handle.
Nights, a demon wildcat scratched

and howled on our tin roof fierce
  as a hailstorm while the worthless
      dogs shivered and whined.

      And then there were our trips home
  late from town. At sundown
sudden figures would appear

in our wagon bed—black-robed,
   faceless—weighing us down so
      the mule team frothed to pull us

      free across that haunted bridge.
  Truth can be rough or polished.
Like a hickory handle, these

tales wear a smidgen thinner,
   shinier with each use. Now
      at the old homeplace, daylight

      leaks through cracks in the clapboards
  wider than before. In each room
a bare bulb swings, opaque

as memory on a charged string,
      a corpse. Now in all the house,
            only a ratty feather tick,

            the cold cook stove. And yet
      smell of fresh biscuits. Clatter
of pail. Want is the mother

of belief. And what, my child,
      do you know of want? Of want
            for milk or second helpings?

            For new shoes, or any shoes?
      For a tight house, a good roof,
indoor plumbing, light after

darkness? To be five and wanting
      a doll, wanting your mother
            to wake from her too-long sleep,

            wanting her voice to be real
      and anchored to her breathing
body? I tell these stories

in hopes you tremble. In hopes
      you realize: Something's coming
            always for your tender soul.

Libby Falk Jones

Dancing Villanelle

My first line needs a partner—what to do?
(Obsession's key, or so the experts say.)
Monsieur, may I have this dance with you?

Perhaps we'll choose a waltz, a rhythm true.
(It helps to relish words, to love to play.)
My first line needs a partner—what to do?

My mama loved to fox trot, Daddy too.
(Take one line at a time, you'll make your way.)
Madame, may I have this dance with you?

A rhumba, or a tango, yes, those two—
(Oh, it's so hard to find the words to say!)
My first line needs a partner—what to do?

Two left feet? —but still, you can dance true.
(Return, return again, this time to stay.)
Mam'selle, may I have this dance with you?

Turns out I like to ville-dance—who knew?
(I think I just could write like this all day.)
My first line's found a partner—we can do,
Monsieur. Merci. Now au revoir to you!

Jessica L. Walsh

Review of the Book I had to Stop Reading at Page 13
--for SD

I can't tell you how I know
you wrote it under fluorescent lights

in uncarpeted rooms
to the sound of a TV no one's watching
or willing to turn off

You wrote it on a street
where a car broke down
and men stood at its engine

and at a bus stop in cold spring
where a woman breathed only in sighs.

And you wrote it to knife my palm
so we could shake bloody hands

unsure at first why we met
skeptical of our tired pleas to God
who seems to have promised our bodies
to the rooms of weeping.

Jed Myers

Quick Gift

The flight just two hours plus, we've traveled
how many lives to this beach? We two
the latest in our long lines, we've made it

down the gauntlet of orbits and out
onto this crust in the ultraviolet,
onto this warm sand in the sun,

these minutes before we climb the steps
into the restaurant with a view for lunch.
I do not feel thankful but giddy

with a moment's advantage, still not gouged
or unspun. I had a spell on the plane.
Blood sank out of my head down the jugular

drains. Something had slowed my heart.
We'll never know what. Went faint, broke a sweat,
couldn't talk, scared my poor companion

half-insane, but she punched the overhead
button, waved, called out…someone came.

Bit of oxygen out of the sudden green
tank on my lap, hit of cranberry juice,
Italian cookie, and I was myself.

Landed, rolled out the rented compact
and on to our Spanish villa facsimile,
and here we've strolled a mile of strand

to sit facing the sea. Moon high
in the blue east widened past half, a translucent
scrap of linen. Horizon studded

with equidistant dark rigs. And we listen
to the twin musics, beach road's traffic
surges and the surf's bursts. We hear

from home the kid's dad is sick in his gut
but we can't learn enough. He doesn't pick up
the phone. We hear from Cleveland, her stepdad's

been taken for tests. Why can't he walk?
There in the scatter of small sticks shells
and pebbles between us, my hand detects

a stone, ovoid, indented. It fits
in my palm and I lift it, look at it, sand-colored

silence—its several grooves of erosion
might well have taken the ocean millennia
rubbing in,

                    and a hole
worn clear through the stone's inch-or-so
width. Of this puzzle I make a quick gift.

She holds it up to her eye, looks my way
through the mineral ring, and laughs,
I suppose, at the curl of weird luck on my lips.

Second Place 2019 Joy Bale Boone Poetry Prize

Hannah Yoest

Sonset

Welcome to McDonalds
    may I take your pulse?

I'd like a number three please,
with a side of milk and honey.

"Jesus is the Sonrise!"
          declares the exchange-

able letter board in front of the church.
    The promise of ecstasy is outlined in neon

next door.
    Rusted exhaust pipes

form an organ. Count your sins
        like pomegranate seeds.

Every legend carries a wooden bat.
    The shadows are already longer than Sunday

service. The pollen valley closes
      your throat. You loosen your collar.

Would you like fries with that?
    Quality without question is a tyrant's

promise to a houseguest. The billboards wink
        and try to sell milk to stray cats.

Fire ants overrun the Easter egg hunt.
      The sun only sets here after it has left

the sky raspberried and bruised.

Chera Hammons

Pegasus

The neighbors' miniature donkey comes visiting
in the summer mornings, his teacup hooves
slipping on asphalt that has started to warm,
loosening the sharp rocks from the tar. When they come
with a bucket of oats to retrieve him,
they can't pull him away from where he stands
and stares at my Haflinger mare.
He plants his feet and gazes up at her,
the colossus of our pasture,
that cascade of cream mane, bright white blaze, golden flank.
The sun behind her. Enrapture. She is like a prophecy
and he is the chosen one who hears it.
He ducks their ropes, just out of reach.
The neighbors always apologize for the donkey
after we help them get him cornered, caught;
they tie him to their truck, drive off slowly,
and we stand admiring his stubbornness,
the angrily shaking head, the flicked-back ears,
and the determined lean toward what he is leaving,
until they are out of sight.
His frustration: that he is not smarter
than mankind, stronger than its machines.
We don't mind the little donkey's tarriances.
Other people's cats kill our quail,
and other people's dogs carry our belongings off.
But the miniature jack only dreams,
and my mare forgets all about him once he is gone,
despite his bravery, his risk, their noses touching through our fence.
Carried in that small heart, some instinct tells him
this journey is one worth taking because
there is something dear within it,
though the best of his hope comes to nothing each day.
No—there is something else he knows, too—
That no beast could be less burdened than one
who believes he owes nothing to his home.

Jayne Marek

Light of Speech

if you will sit with me in the light
of speech, I will sit with you…
                —A. R. Ammons

we want to believe in the persistence of caterpillars' slow climb
toward their leafy meals, their bodies squirming hieroglyphs

at the end of silk filaments, and the ever-returning honeysuckle
vines opening orange trumpets in a garden, and a towhee

mewing as it rustles in dry duff day after day for seeds
and insects and spiders, and spiders themselves which express

an exacting grasp of physics and geometry as they set
the anchor points of their webs to surfaces sometimes widely

separated and buffed by winds (the spiders' worlds arguably
as complex as ours, and more precise in their expression

than the words we often let ourselves get away with
as supposedly educated modern humans) since persistence

and precision are built into nature's way and yet are not
always ascendant: the configuration of human language

resides in this same paradox, the rose by any other name
being the rose that is a rose that is a rose, that is,

meanings are in some ways accidental; any one sound
or signal, to be understood, must be understood against

the backdrop of a pattern, yet describing a complicated
emotional wholeness remains a challenge for us language-

bound creatures: when, enjoying a summer morning, one hears
the thump of an unwary chickadee against a pane of glass

and sees it lying on the ground, more tiny than it appeared
when lively and bustling and arguing with its mixed flock

of foragers about what there is to eat in the back yard,
now hunched, its head twisted to one side in the posture

of death that signals it has begun its own return to
the natural order of decay, and in the meanwhile its copper

and black and white feathers stilled in the grass
that slowly lifts its blade tips as it recovers from the bird's

body landing, then an observer may ponder the difficulty
of expressing this minuscule event that is both great and small:

what is the significance of this happening, that is,
for whom can the death of the chickadee convey a distinct

message (how abrupt one's end can be, how it changes
the atmosphere of the morning into a mourning)?

I take a lesson from the single curled white breast feather
still afloat after the bird's fall, like a fragment of cirrus:

existence expresses itself through our forms and movements,
our bodily speech takes us precisely toward our endings:

if sometimes we make light of our oncoming end,
nevertheless there is continuance:

the dead bird's feathers shine in morning light
and the tiny body expresses the world and more

Christina Seymour

Nothing like an End

The doubt began with ambiguity—
a question you tactfully ignored,
your dizzying, splendid shirt
suggesting finality, the way fluorescents
light and unlight the small bar,
light and unlight the fried woman soaked from rain.
That was a door sound, you say, looking up
toward a creak. I say, That was weird, or rad,
or something else that doesn't encompass it.
Again, I say doubt in the mirror
in the morning brushing my teeth,
then, again, at night—is it mindful or mindless,
the repetitive daily motion—this questioning,
the pulsing light from the storm
like a dirge in the eardrum. My face distorted, too.

Younger Artists

Mason Thomas

Naming My Future Daughter

As someone who herself was named for her father's dead sister, I know the kinds of legacies a name can leave. In the Bible, Deborah was the only female judge of Israel, the first feminist in a book where most women are referred to as "the wife of". In Judges 5 you can read The Song of Deborah and it is a victory hymn. I will tell you that I did not feel victorious on the playground when the boys called me De-boring for wanting to read instead of play kickball.

My mom always wanted to name her daughter Lillian after her grandmother, but when I came along, my dad wanted to name me after his sister. They compromised and named me after his sister, but my mom got to pick my middle name which I would go by. She loved the name Mason because it meant strong after the stonemasons. The stonemasons were builders. They laid brick after brick to create houses, and freed statues from their marble confines. I may not work with stone, but I build my stories out of syllables and I write words that live outside of pages. My name may not be common among girls, but I don't have to be a boy to live a strong life. I can be five foot six and still stand up for myself. I can be a poet who failed math and still know who I am.

This, this name is my home. My name is the armor that I lace up and also the sword that the world can use to pierce me. My name is the way that I love myself. My name woos me flowers and chocolates and soft blankets. My name is a traitor. My name can make me feel like the most insecure and the most confident person in a room.

I went to school with a girl named Joanna. I'm not sure if her mother named her after the girl in Sweeney Todd or if she wanted her daughter to know that "God is gracious". All I know is that after that senior basketball player bragged about doing her in the locker room her name became Hoe-anna. Her identity was stripped from her just like the jeans she was wearing. Her name was no longer her person-hood, but something twisted and held against her, so pardon me if I have a list that is pages long of baby names because I have to ridicule every person that my daughter might become. Because I know that her name will not be her property, it will be ammunition for the people that want to hurt her.

It will be shortened and lengthened, chopped into pieces and used for spare parts to please the eyes of her beholders. When the world splays her ribcage apart like a butterfly, takes a melon-baller and scoops out her very substance, the same thing it does to so many of its daughters, what will she be left with? When she is no longer a person, but a thing to be toyed with, a thing to be ogled, who will she be?

I've always loved the name Indigo for a daughter but my sister laughed and told me that naming my kid after a crayola crayon was stupid. I tried to tell her that I wasn't naming her after a crayon, I was naming her for the way the sky looks at dusk. I was naming her for the color of the shirt her father wore when we met. I was naming her for the Indigo plant that survives the coldest winters and still blooms in the spring, the plant that has been known to heal pain, so that maybe, by looking at my daughter, I'll forget about the now empty half of my bed.

The first thing we do with our daughters in this world is cry. When I brush my fingertips underneath my little girl's eyes I'll say Baby. Mothers have tasted their daughters tears for centuries. The crook of my elbow was made to hold your head high when you can't. My palms have walked you across streets and parking lots. I don't mind walking you through heartbreak. Baby girl, you have wisdom in your name. You are known for your rarity and the world has always thought you were precious. You are a part of the rainbow, you are nature's creation, you are you. And that's always who I wanted you to be.

Ashley Taylor

The Church on Shoal Creek Rd.

You know that something awful's happened here
some years and months and days ago, before
piano hymns spilled over a leaf-strewn floor,
a plea for the people to reappear.

The rafters arc like ribs rubbed raw by time,
remembering the stares of those who turned
their eyes to search for the Divine, who yearned
for purpose in these rafters choked by grime.

The mice write dissonant compositions
in A and G minor, plucking on strings
that used to play the Psalms and King of Kings,
dancing across the keys like tone-deaf musicians.

The stained-glass saints cast light around the room
through holey robes with edges pointing like teeth,
the shards tossed onto well-worn pews a wreath
of glowing flowers thrown upon a tomb.

The ghost of worship marks the walls in white,
where crosses hung for years above the doors
and awed footfalls wore paths along the floors,
marks left by those who saw a thing finite.

The memory of people singing
remains inside the old piano's wood
after the people have all gone and stood
in other churches, other bells ringing.

Ashley Taylor

Fall in E Major

The fields that nurture people,
as well as golden corn and winter wheat,
surround houses like a brown blanket
after combines shift the soil.
Cows sing into the twilight,
after farmers have gone to bed,
swishing grass between their legs
as deer unfold themselves from swaying trees.
Does dance through pastures while bucks
leap behind, antlers scraping sky.
Coyotes strike up a harmony,
their laughter floating like the stars
underneath a Harvest Moon.
Owls swoop, wheel a hush upon the land,
with wings like heaven and talons like hell.
Cows low to herald the returning sun,
coaxing birds to flock in a periwinkle sky.
Coyotes evaporate, like dew;
Deer bow back to lay their heads
where night still clings among the trees, under sheltering leaves.
The warm and living earth breathes life into the day,
farmers waking to shift the soil again,
mixing the nighttime song with the clay.

Coleman Bomar

Bird Born Between

Born a bird
But
Bred a boy.

They clipped pink wings
And plucked feathers from my groin.

You will be Man they said,
Chirping sterile disdain.

Surgical masks like white beaks
Mocking mine removed.

Flying is not for you they said,
Shearing peacock from pockmarked skin.

Love for the sky only grew with age
And I would try feathers which suited me.

Made a man
But
Meant a macaw

I am a boy
And
I am a bird
So
I am an angel.

Born to fly even if it means
Falling.

Elli McMillen

Prettier

Did you
Hear what he said

                  Oh, I can't imagine

Said I'd be prettier

                  Prettier How?

Said I'd be prettier if I smiled
More.
As if somehow a pearlescent flash of teeth
Symbolizes happiness gladness beauty and
Makes another feel warm.
Makes them feel good   inside.
But it makes me not so.

                  Pray now, may our voices be heard
Like a show-pony, heralded around to incite
Feelings of pleasure and warmth within a man.
To scrape his opinions down the faces of women
As if somehow his suggestion states a superior smart.
    As if somehow he knows how women feel
      How every single person feels.
I wonder if, like me, he ever experiences sonder

Maybe then he wouldn't
Go around demanding smiles the way you might demand change.
Change to spill out from an activist vending machine that just keeps
Taking all of our money
And throwing it into the hands of famous victims
Who brand us as the falsifiers.

But, sure, tell me to smile more.
It's the least of your worries.
            This all started with an unwelcome suggestion?

Michael Westerfield

Jack's Art

Some leaves of October are
finally turning and falling
not from chill but hot boredom.

Rainbow helicopter blades crash
Wobble, spin, paper airplane glide to
crash atop grass still too green

Dried by the sun, burning
Until chopped and mulched
hide bugs from lingering robins.

Pearl lined spider webs made
heavy with dew drop jewelry
sag exhausted by the burden.

Baked leaves shatter beneath
a hail storm of over ripe acorns and
cannonball walnuts.

All await the announcement
of autumn's late arrival
ushering summer away.

Late tomatoes and okra
long for winter sleep
in jars or in flash frozen darkness.

Cattle dust themselves beneath trees
Try to discourage summer swarms
as deer panting on shaded hillsides

too hot to fight and breed.
Life cycle on hold longer still
Wipe sweat and swat mosquitoes

When will etch-a-sketch artwork
deck crisp pond edges and
garden shed windowpanes?

Caitie Mihelic

Society Strangles

I feel strangled

        Society has me trapped

I struggle to grasp

        My strength is sapped

I tried to be beautiful

        Long luscious dark curls
A slim petite form

        Still just an empty girl

I feel the sweat trickle

        From too much weight
Its heavy to hold

        Is this my fate?

I stand completely bare

        Yet much more complete
I should be scared

        This isn't my utter defeat

Hunter Rissmann

Skin Art Museum

Bodies as canvases,

        a very cliché idea.

  Would you peel your skin off

    to hang on display?

I didn't think so.

  Some pieces are sacred--

The footprints of an unborn child on a wrist.

  A two-headed snake slithering down a forearm.

    The name of an ex-lover displayed in Old English on an ass.

These acquisitions of body art followed by constant:

  "You know that's permanent right?"

      Or

  "Why would you get that?"

  No matter how you look at it,
It is permanent.

    That's okay though.

You must be decisive about something.

Jaren Childers

The Special Fruit Packed in My Lunchbox with Love

The first bite frustrates
the taste buds and makes
my cheeks tingle.

My body craved
something crunchy
like a Kiku apple.

Juice droplets dribble down
fingers to my wrist.

The inside coats my
caramel-colored hands
and to-do list.

The sound and crispness
of each bite remind
me of fireworks.

The loud munch
makes my shoulders quirk.

Out of the hole
pokes a green worm.

While the class read,
I stared at the calendar.

Apples were my
childhood, for the fruit
represented teaching.

I'd open my lunchbox
to a vivid, red delicious apple
and a note from my mother
with a smiley face, winking.

LaNina Jones

Just As They Were

When people speak my name, I
want to be remembered as Athena
was.

A mediator, someone who used her words as
her weapon to make a change. Just as Apollo was,

I want to be remembered for loving the world and
the arts we used to create it. Just as Apollo
was,

I want to be engulfed in my sorrow, my anger, my heart,
and create art that will be just as Athena was,

Powerful, moving, burned in the minds of those who
 will be left to tell my tale. Just as Athena was

able to move mountains and stand her ground in the
face of man, I want to be just as Athena
was.

I want to create a world where people use the arts to make
their statement and to be looked to for answers, just as Apollo was.

To be looked upon by the golden sun and the
one who dared to be different, just as Apollo was.

The pen is my lyre, the canvas my aegis, and
I will be strong and brilliant, just as they were.

Biographies

In his later years **Gary Beaumier** has become a beachcomber. On a number of occasions he has constructed wooden sailboats. He is a finalist for the Luminaire Award and nominated for the Best of the Net Award.

Coleman Bomar is a young writer who enjoys growing in his craft. His writing explores elements of philosophy, religion, surrealism and odd life experiences. When he is not sleeping, one can find him watching a bad movie, reading a good book, or walking in the woods.

Jaren Childers is a sophomore at ECTC. She is involved in many extra curricular activities in addition to creative writing, having recently played Tituba in a local production of *The Crucible*.

Linda Flaherty Haltmaier is an award-winning author and the Poet Laureate of Andover, Massachusetts. She is the winner of the Homebound Publications Poetry Prize for her full-length collection, *Rolling up the Sky* (2016). Her latest collection *To the Left of the Sun* was released in August, 2018 by Homebound Publications. Her poetry has been nominated for a Pushcart Prize and has appeared extensively in journals and anthologies.

Chera Hammons' work has appeared in *Beloit Poetry Journal, Rattle, THRUSH, Tupelo Quarterly,* and *Valparaiso Poetry Review.* Her most recent book, *The Traveler's Guide to Bomb City,* received the 2017 PEN Southwest Book Award. She lives in Amarillo, TX.

LaNina Jones is ready to transfer to Western Kentucky University to pursue her degree in Secondary Education as an English intsructor. She is the recipient of ECTC's 2019 Humanities Award.

Libby Falk Jones is the author of a chapbook, *Above the Eastern Treetops, Blue* (Finishing Line, 2010) and co-author of *Balance of Five* (Berea, 2015). Professor Emerita of English at Berea College where she taught creative writing, Jones is a member of Bluegrass Writers Studio and a past president of Kentucky State Poetry Society.

Michael Lasater is a professor, musician, filmmaker and artist. He has performed with ensembles including the Metropolitan Opera, produced documentaries on poetry, and currently exhibits art video internationally. His poetry has appeared in *Heartland!* and *Kansas Time + Place.*

Jayne Marek's poetry appears in *Cortland Review, Raven Chronicles, Women's Studies Quarterly, Spillway, Notre Dame Review,* and many other journals. Twice nominated for a Pushcart Prize, she has two chapbooks, one co-authored poetry collection, and two full-length poetry books.

Elli McMillen is a Maryville College senior majoring in English Literature and minoring in both Art and Spanish. Elli is fascinated with language and loves to play with words, both in structure and meaning, through writing or through the books she's constantly reading. Alongside a newfound interest in writing, Elli also enjoys painting and dabbling in the creative arts.

Tim Menees grew up in Seattle. He moved to Pittsburgh where he drew editorial cartoons at the city's morning paper for 30 years. His work appeared in national newspapers and news magazines. Today he draws cartoons and writes for *The Pittsburgh Quarterly*, paints and plays the piano.

Jed Myers is author of *Watching the Perseids* (winner of the Sacramento Poetry Center Book Award), *The Marriage of Space and Time* (MoonPath Press), and four chapbooks, including *Dark's Channels* (winner of the *Iron Horse Literary Review* Chapbook Award) and *Love's Test* (winner of the Grayson Books Chapbook Competition, forthcoming). Among other recognitions, Jed is Poetry Editor for the journal *Bracken*.

Hunter Rissman is a sophomore at Elizabethtown Community and Technical College.

Christina Seymour is the author of *When is a Burning Tree* (Glass Lyre Press 2018) and the chapbook *Flowers Around Your Soft Throat* (Structo 2016). Her poems also appear in *The Moth*, *North American Review*, *Cimarron Review*, Wick Poetry Center's exhibit, *Speak Peace—American Voices Respond to Vietnamese Children's Paintings*, and elsewhere. Her work received the Russell MacDonald Creative Writing Award and has been nominated for the Pushcart Prize, Best New Poets, and the AWP Intro Award.

Patrick Sylvain is a poet, social critic, and photographer. Twice nominated for the Pushcart Prize, his work can be found in several creative anthologies and reviews, including: *African American Review*, *Agni*, *American Poetry Review*, *Aperture*, *Callaloo*, *Caribbean Writers*, *Transition*, *Ploughshares*, *SX Salon*, *The Oxford Book of Caribbean Verse*. Sylvain is on faculty at Brown University's Africana Studies. Sylvain is also the Shirle Dorothy Robbins Creative Writing Prize Fellow at Brandeis University.

Ashley Taylor studied Creative Writing at Murray State University, graduating with a Bachelor's degree. She writes flash fiction and creative nonfiction in between job interviews and traveling. Taylor enjoys works that explore the fantastic and challenge the ordinary.

Mason Thomas is a 21-year-old English major at Elizabethtown Community and Technical College. She will graduate this spring with the hopes of having a career in writing and possibly continuing her education at the University of Louisville. She is the recipient of ECTC's 2019 Fine Arts Award.

Kory Wells is a poet, writer, storyteller, and advocate for the arts. She is the author of Sugar Fix, forthcoming from Terrapin Books, and Heaven Was the Moon, a poetry chapbook from March Street Press. In 2017 she was selected the inaugural Poet Laureate of Murfreesboro, TN. Her work has appeared in numerous online and print publications, including *Helen, James Dickey Review, Ruminate, Stirring,* and *The Southern Poetry Anthology*.

Jessica L. Walsh is the author of two poetry collections, How to Break My Neck and The List of Last Tries (forthcoming 2019), as well as two chapbooks. Her work has appeared in *RHINO, Tinderbox, Glass: A Poetry Journal*, and more. She is a community college professor and the blog manager for Agape Editions.

Michael Westerfield is a Mississippi native who served 20 years as an Army photojournalist. His goal for a second career is to be a freelance writer, poet and author. He is currently working on his first novel and several other projects. He hopes that his works help others see God at work in their lives, to recognize and appreciate the big miracles and the little ones.

Hannah Yoest is a writer and editor for a weekly magazine in Washington D.C. Her poetry is forthcoming in several literary magazines this fall. She is a graduate of the University of Virginia where she studied fine art photography. She studied poetry at the Iowa Writers Workshop summer course and has attended the VQR writers' conference. She is also an artist in residence at the ceramics studio KUZEH Pottery. You can find her on instagram: https://www.instagram.com/avecruth/ and twitter: https://twitter.com/ruthyoest

CPSIA information can be obtained
at www.ICGtesting.com
Printed in the USA
LVHW030523080519
617017LV00009B/92

9 780999 686850